The Gross Book of Jokes

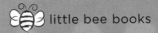

An imprint of Bonnier Publishing Group
853 Broadway, New York, New York 10003
Copyright © 2014 by Igloo Books Ltd.
This little bee books edition, 2015.
All rights reserved, including the right of
reproduction in whole or in part in any form.
LITTLE BEE BOOKS is a trademark of
Bonnier Publishing Group, and
associated colophon is a trademark of
Bonnier Publishing Group.

Manufactured in China LEO002 0715
First Edition 2 4 6 8 10 9 7 5 3 1
ISBN 978-1-4998-0162-0

www.littlebeebooks.com
www.bonnierpublishing.com

The Gross Book of Jokes

little bee books

THIS BOOK BELONGS TO:

....

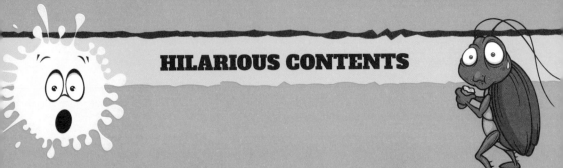

HILARIOUS CONTENTS

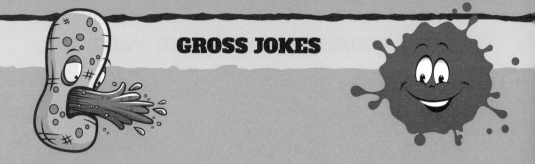

GROSS JOKES

We're going to tell you such hilarious, gross, disgusting, yucky, revolting, and horrible jokes that you will laugh until you really need to pee. That is our mission and we choose to accept it.

Has it been a while since you have been completely and utterly grossed out? Well, that is about to change. Not only will the jokes in this book disgust you in ways you didn't even know you could be disgusted, but you can then tell them to others to disgust them. Sound good?

We all know that the best jokes are the most disgusting ones, and we plan to tell you only the best jokes.

With fart jokes, burp jokes, smelly jokes, slimy jokes, monster jokes, and toilet jokes, this book has it all.

Prepare yourself for what is about to happen. Take a deep breath (sorry about the smell, I just farted), relax, and ignore the hairy spider crawling down your leg. Get ready to get gross.

Did You Know?

It has been proven that gross jokes are 98% more likely to make you throw up than non-gross jokes.

Mommy, Mommy, can I lick the bowl?

No, just flush like everyone else does.

CAN YOU SMELL THAT?

Everybody loves a good smelly joke. So come on and take a good sniff. There's something really disgusting in the air.

What did one smelly sock say to the other smelly sock?

"Are you stinking what I'm stinking?"

What's big and gray and stinks?

A smellyphant.

What's icky, yellow, and smells like bananas?

Monkey vomit.

What do you call a fairy who hasn't taken a bath?

Stinkerbell.

What's wet and brown and smells like peanuts?

Elephant puke.

A boy walks into a shop with a big pile of dog poop in his hand. He looks at the shopkeeper and says, "Phew. Look at that. To think I nearly stepped in it."

CAN YOU SMELL THAT?

What did one eye say to the other eye?

"Between you and me, something smells."

Tony had to go to the doctor because every time he tried to speak, he farted.

"You must help me, doctor. It's so embarrassing. The only good thing is that my farts don't smell."

"Hmmmm," said the doctor. "I will have to send you to a specialist."

"A bottom specialist or a surgeon?" asked Tony.

"Neither," said the doctor. "I'm sending you to a nose specialist. There's clearly something very wrong with yours."

A belch is just one
gust of wind,
that comes straight
from the heart,
but should it take the
downward route,
It turns into a fart.

What happens when
you play table tennis
with a rotten egg?

First it goes ping, then
it goes pong.

What's the smelliest
city in America?

Poo York.

How many rotten
eggs does it take to
make a stink bomb?

A phew.

What's the sharpest thing in the world?

A fart. It goes through your pants and doesn't even leave a hole.

Doug: "My dog's got no nose."

Matt: "How does he smell?"

Doug: "Just awful."

Why do giraffes have such long necks?

Because they have smelly feet.

GROSS JOKES

What is the smelliest queen in the world called?

The Queen of Farts.

Did you hear the joke about the fart?

You don't want to. It stinks.

What did the skunk say when the wind changed direction?

"It's all coming back to me now."

CAN YOU SMELL THAT?

What's green and smelly?

The Incredible Hulk when he farts.

"Doctor, doctor, I'm going bald. Do you have anything to cure it?"

"Yes, put one pound of horse poop on your head every single morning."

"Will that make my hair grow back?"

"No, but no one will come close enough to see that you don't have any hair."

What's brown and smelly and sits on a piano stool?

Beethoven's last movement.

16

Did you hear about the slow student with terrible gas?

He was getting farter and farter behind, so his parents hired a tooter.

What's round, white, stinky, and giggly?

A tickled onion.

What's the best way to keep flies out of your bathroom?

Poop in the hallway.

On what day of the week do most people get diarrhea?

Splatter-day.

CAN YOU SMELL THAT?

Where do burgers go to dance?

A meat ball.

What's invisible and smells like carrots?

Bunny farts.

If you are in an assembly, and your bottom wants to shout, whatever you do, don't let it out.

GROSS JOKES

What smells, runs around all day, and lies around at night with its tongue hanging out?

A pair of old sneakers.

What's green and smells?

An alien's nose.

What do you get if you cross a skunk with an owl?

Something that smells, but doesn't give a hoot.

SLIMY

Slime is funny. Don't ask why.
It just is. Slugs and slime go together
like poop and farts. Now that's gross.
Don't even get us started on snot.

What did the
slug say as he slid
down the wall?

"How slime flies."

Why was the
nose tired?

Because it never
stopped running.

GROSS JOKES

What did the slug say to the other slug who had hit him and run away?

"I'll get you next slime."

What did the spider say to the slug?

"It's about slime you showed up."

Anna thought the green flecks on the wall were paint.

Now we know it's snot.

How do you know your kitchen floor is dirty?

The slugs leave a trail on the floor that reads *clean me*.

SLIMY

What do you do when two snails have a fight?

Leave them to slug it out.

What is the difference between a prince and a booger?

The prince is the heir to the throne, but the booger is thrown to the air.

How do snails get their shells so shiny?

They use snail varnish.

How do you cure dandruff?

Cut off your head.

GROSS JOKES

What is the definition of a slug?

A snail with a housing problem.

Don't kiss your honey, when your nose is runny.
You may think it's funny, but it's snot.

What was the snail doing on the road?

About one mile a day.

What do blobs like to drink the most?

Slime-ade.

How do you stop a cold from going to your chest?

Tie a knot in your neck.

Why did the booger cross the road?

He was getting picked on.

What kind of bugs live in clocks?

Ticks.

What's another name for a snail?

A booger wearing a crash helmet.

What should you do if your nose goes on strike?

Picket.

What did the boy maggot say to the girl maggot?

"What's a nice girl like you doing in a joint like this?"

GROSS JOKES

Why was the glow-worm confused?

She didn't know if she was coming or glowing.

How do you make a tissue dance?

Put a little booger into it.

What is gross, slimy, and stuck between sharks' teeth?

Slow swimmers.

27

SLIMY

What's green and wobbly and hangs from trees?

Monkey snot.

Why do gorillas have big nostrils?

Because they have big fingers.

What is it called when someone gets hit in the face with slime?

Goo-lash.

Aaron: "Did you just pick your nose?"

Doug: "No, I was born with it."

GROSS JOKES

Why do basketball players carry handkerchiefs?

They're always dribbling.

What is a cow's snot called?

Moo-cus.

Why do bees have sticky hair?

Because they use honey combs.

MONSTER JOKES

Monsters don't have to be scary. Instead, they can be hilarious. From Dr. Frankenstein to the Loch Ness Monster, let's poke fun at some terrifying creatures.

What's grosser than three dead monsters in a trash can?

One dead monster in three trash cans.

What do you call a monster with no neck?

The Lost Neck Monster.

What happened when the alien ate uranium?

He got atomic ache.

GROSS JOKES

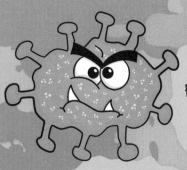

How did Frankenstein's monster sit in a chair?

Bolt upright.

Why did Frankenstein's monster get indigestion?

He bolted down his food.

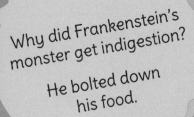

Why is it foolish to upset a cannibal?

You will find yourself in hot water.

MONSTER JOKES

Why did the monster eat the North Pole?

He was in the mood for a frozen dinner.

Which monster makes strange noises in its throat?

A gargoyle.

Why didn't the skeleton want to go bungee jumping?

Because he didn't have the guts.

What would you get if you crossed a practical joker with a mad scientist?

Dr. Prankenstein.

What do you call a corpse who won't stop ringing your doorbell?

A dead ringer.

What did the cannibal say to her kids at the dinner table?

"Don't talk with people in your mouth."

What do cannibals do at a wedding?

Toast the bride and groom.

MONSTER JOKES

Why did the alien
have a bath?

So he could make
a clean getaway.

How can you help
a starving cannibal?

Give him a hand.

Who created
the fowlest monster
in the world?

Ducktor Frankenstein.

What's green
and fluffy and comes
from Mars?

A martianmallow.

Why is Frankenstein's
monster such a
good gardener?

Because he has
green fingers.

Why are most mummies vain and conceited?

They're all wrapped up in themselves.

How does a cannibal greet a guest?

"Pleased to eat you."

What do you call a scary movie about a monster who takes money?

The Bribe of Frankenstein.

MONSTER JOKES

Monster: "Will this hurt?"

Dr. Frankenstein: "Let's just say you're in for a big shock."

What did the cannibal say after he ate the circus clown?

"Boy, that sure tasted funny."

What type of music does a mummy like the most?

Wrap.

What did one casket say to the other?

"Is that you, coffin?"

Was Dracula ever married?

No, he was a bat-chelor.

36

GROSS JOKES

What do you get when you cross a ghost with a firecracker?

Bam-boo.

Did you hear about the monster with five legs?

No, but I bet his pants fit him like a glove.

Where do baby monsters go when their parents are at work?

Day scare.

What do big, scary monsters do to cars?

They make traffic jam.

Why are skeletons calm?

Because nothing gets under their skin.

What do prophetic ghosts like reading?

Horror-scopes.

Where should a greedy, 500-pound monster go?

On a diet.

GROSS JOKES

What do baby ghosts play with?

Deady bears.

Why are graveyards noisy?

Because of all the coffin.

What type of fruit do vampires like the most?

Neck-tarines.

39

GRIMY AND SICK

Some subjects are gross and grimy. They can be sticky and icky or gross and dirty. Puke is all of those things at the same time. Eeewww!

Birdy, birdy, in the sky, dropped some white stuff in my eye. I'm a big boy, I won't cry. I'm just glad that cows don't fly.

A minister was asked to dinner by one of his parishioners, whom he knew was an unkempt housekeeper. When he sat down at the table, he noticed that the dishes were the dirtiest dishes he had ever seen.

"Were these dishes ever washed?" he asked his hostess, running his fingers over the grit and grime.

She replied, "They're as clean as soap and water could get them."

He felt quite apprehensive, but, not wanting to offend, he blessed the food anyway and started eating. It was really delicious and he said so, despite the dirty dishes.

When dinner was over, the hostess took the dishes to the dogs outside and yelled, "Here, Soap. Here, Water."

What's brown and sticky?

A stick.

What is red with green spots?

I don't know, but whatever it is, it just crawled behind your ear.

GRIMY AND SICK

Why do gross maggots eat vomit?

It's a dirty job, but someone has to do it.

What's yellow and smells of dead humans?

Cannibal puke.

What has four legs, a tail, and flies?

A dead horse.

Why do mother birds puke in their babies' mouths?

They want to send them out with a hot breakfast.

Mom: "Why did you put a frog in your sister's bed?"

John: "I couldn't find a snake."

What's brown and sounds like a bell?

Dung.

What's Mozart doing in his grave?

He's de-composing.

Why were the teacher's eyes crossed?

She couldn't control her pupils.

What did the man say when his vomit missed the bucket?

"Now that's beyond the pail."

What do you get when you put your grandpa in the freezer?

A popsicle.

What kind of cake do you get at a bad cafe?

A stomach-cake.

What do you call a surgeon with eight arms?

A doctopus.

GROSS JOKES

What shouldn't you drink when you have the flu?

Cough-ee.

What TV show did the puke like to watch?

Wallace and Vomit.

What do you call a crazy flea?

A loony-tic.

What illness do martial artists get?

Kung Flu.

What sound does a nut make when it sneezes?

"Cashew."

What did one elevator say to the other elevator?

"I think I'm coming down with something."

What time should you visit the dentist?

Tooth-hurty.

Dave: "Sir, my nose is running."

Teacher: "Well, chase after it."

Why did the bird go to the hospital?

To get tweeted.

GROSS JOKES

What did the chicken say when it laid a square egg?

"Ouch."

How does a pig get to the hospital?

In a hambulance.

What do you call a dog with the runs?

A poodle.

47

GRIMY AND SICK

Did you hear about the bird that acts crazy?

He's stork raving mad.

What did the dentist ask her husband when he baked a cake?

"Can I do the filling?"

How do you fix a broken tomato?

With tomato paste.

What do you give a dog with a fever?

Mustard. It's the best thing for a hot dog.

Why did the banana peel?

Because it didn't wear sunscreen.

Patient: "Doctor, doctor, I swallowed food dye."

Doctor: "You'll be okay."

Patient: "I feel like I've dyed a little inside."

What's in space, has feathers, and farts a lot?

An Unidentified Farting Ostrich.

What did the astronaut call his poo in outer space?

A floater.

Why didn't the girl tell the doctor that she ate some glue?

Her lips were sealed.

49

GROSS TONGUE-TWISTERS

These tongue-twisters will have
your tongue going in all directions.
They are not like the jokes in the rest
of this book, but they will sound funny
and silly. And when you think about the
words, you might get grossed out.
You'll definitely have to reach into
your mouth and untwist your tongue.

Six slippery snails
slid slowly seaward.

I need not your needles,
they're needless to me,
for kneading of noodles was
needless, you see.

Did my pretty pants need to
be kneed? I then should have
need of your needles indeed.

Freshly fried fat flying fish.

If a black bug bleeds black blood, what blood does a blue bug bleed?

A skunk sat on a stump and the stump thought the skunk stunk. The skunk thought the stump stunk. So, what stunk: the skunk or the stump?

The ochre ogre ogled the poker.

How many seals did the seal slicer slice since the seal slicer shan't slice slippery seals?

Which rich wicked witch wished a wicked wish about another rich wicked witch?

GROSS JOKES

I stepped on a stump and stomped on it, then I had a scratch that turned into a sore.

I feel a funny feeling. A funny feeling I feel. If you feel the feeling I feel, then I feel the feeling you feel.

A big, black bug bit a big, black bear and the big, black bear bled blood.

If Stu chews shoes, should Stu choose the shoes he chews?

Andrew and Arthur ate awful, acidic apples accidentally.

Francis fries foul fish fillets.

Brad's big, black bath brush broke.

Betty Botter had some butter. "This butter's bitter," she said. "If I bake this bitter butter, it would make my batter bitter, but a bit of better butter, that would make my batter better."

The rat-catchers can't catch caught rats.

If Freaky Fred found fifty feet of fruit and fed forty feet to his friend, Frank, how many feet of fruit did Freaky Fred find in the first place?

When a doctor pukes everywhere and another doctor doctors him, does the doctor doing the doctoring have to doctor the doctor the way the doctor being doctored wants to be doctored, or does the doctor doing the doctoring of the doctor doctor the doctor as he wants to do the doctoring?

There was an old lady from Ryde, who drank apple cider and died. The apples fermented, inside the lamented, and made cider inside her insides.

The sloth loafs among the low slopes.

Three fiddling pigs sat in a pit and fiddled.

Fiddle, piggy, fiddle, piggy, fiddle, piggy.

The savor of the silly scent the sentry sent to Millicent.

How many slim, slimy snakes would slither silently to the sea if slim, slimy snakes could slither silently?

Amidst the mists and coldest frosts, with stoutest wrists and loudest boasts, he thrust his fists against the posts, and still insists he sees the ghosts.

Around the rugged rocks the ragged rascal ran.

Plague-bearing prairie dogs. Plague-bearing prairie dogs.

Crisp crusts crackle crunchily.

I cannot bear to see a bear bear down upon a hare. When bare of hair he strips the hare, right there I cry, "Forbear."

Flee from fog to fight flu fast.

Theo's throat throbs and thumps, thumps and throbs.

Many a sea anemone sees an enemy anemone.

Sixty-six sticky skeletons. Sixty-six sticky skeletons. Sixty-six sticky skeletons.

Horrible Heidi hears hairy Horace holler.

She stood on the balcony, inexplicably mimicking him hiccuping and amicably welcoming him home.

The epitome of femininity.

A selfish shellfish smelt a stale fish. If the stale fish was smelt, then the selfish shellfish smelt a smell.

Girl gargoyle, guy gargoyle.

FOOD GONE BAD

Fresh food is delicious, but even delicious food can be made totally, horribly gross. Animals can make a home in your food, and mold can grow in it. Eeeuurrgh!

Why did the jelly wobble?

Because it saw the milk shake.

What's worse than finding a worm in your apple?

Finding half a worm.

GROSS JOKES

Jake: "What's the difference between dog poop and chocolate?"

Mick: "I don't know."

Jake: "In that case, don't ever buy me chocolate."

Waiter: "What will you have to follow the roast pork, sir?"

Alex: "Indigestion, I expect."

Why shouldn't you tell a joke to an egg?

It might crack up.

What's green and red and goes 100 miles an hour?

A frog in a blender.

61

Brian: "Waiter, waiter, I simply can't eat this awful food. Get me the manager."

Waiter: "She won't eat it either."

A family of three tomatoes were walking down the street one day when the little baby tomato started lagging behind. The father tomato walked back to the baby tomato, stomped on her, squashing her into a red paste and said, "Ketch up."

What happened when the waiter tripped while carrying the intestines soup?

He spilled his guts.

What kind of peas are brown?

Poopeas.

What's the difference between a Brussels sprout and a booger?

You can't get a kid to eat a Brussels sprout.

First egg: "I don't want to go in a pan of boiling water."

Second egg: "It gets worse. When they take you out, they bash your head in."

What's yellow and stupid?

Thick custard.

FOOD GONE BAD

Why did the banana go to the doctor?

Because it wasn't peeling well.

A guy walks into the doctor's office. He has a banana stuck in one of his ears, an asparagus stalk in the other ear, and a carrot stuck in one nostril. The man says, "Doctor, this is terrible. What's wrong with me?"

The doctor says, "Well, first of all, you need to eat more sensibly."

First apple: "You look down in the dumps. What's eating you?"

Second apple: "Worms, I think."

Patrick: "Waiter, waiter, be careful! Your thumb is in my soup!"

Waiter: "Not to worry. It isn't very hot."

How do you make a milkshake?

Give it a good scare.

Tom: "Waiter, waiter, this egg is bad."

Waiter: "Don't blame me, I only laid the table."

What can a whole apple do that half an apple can't do?

It can look round.

FOOD GONE BAD

A young man entered the ice cream shop and asked, "What kind of ice cream do you have?"

"Vanilla, chocolate, strawberry," the girl wheezed. She patted her chest and seemed unable to continue.

"Do you have laryngitis?" the young man asked.

"Nope," she whispered. "Just vanilla, chocolate and strawberry."

Harry: "Waiter, waiter, there's a dead beetle in my drink."

Waiter: "Well, yes, the dead ones aren't very good swimmers."

What is the scariest fruit?

A boo-nana.

What did the chewing gum say to the shoe?

"I'm stuck on you."

GROSS JOKES

Why did the students eat their homework?

The teacher said it was a piece of cake.

What does a termite eat for breakfast?

Oak-meal.

What's green and white and jumps up and down?

A frog sandwich.

What fruit juice do ghosts like the most?

Lemon and slime.

What does an anteater like on its pizza?

Ant-chovies.

FOOD GONE BAD

Jack: "Waiter, waiter, there's a cockroach in my salad."

Waiter: "Please don't shout or the other customers will ask for one, too."

Did you hear about the cannibal who was late for lunch?

He was given the cold shoulder.

What do zombies eat for breakfast?

Dreaded Wheat.

Want to hear a joke about pizza?

Never mind. It's too cheesy.

GROSS JOKES

What did one maggot say to the other who was stuck in an apple?

"Try and worm your way out of that one."

Did you hear about the man who put his false teeth in backward?

He ate himself.

Bob: "Waiter, waiter, why is your thumb on my steak?"

Waiter: "I don't want to drop it again."

What's the difference between roast chicken and pea soup?

You can roast chicken, but you can't pea soup.

Why do the French like to eat snails?

Because they don't like fast food.

ANIMAL GROSSNESS

Animals can be really gross, and these jokes will have you and your friends in stitches. They're silly and full of creepy-crawlies and other slithery and smelly animals.

How can you tell when a gorilla's been in the fridge?

There is hair in the butter.

What do you call a bear with its ear cut off?

B.

What do you get if you cross a fish with a pig?

Wet and dirty.

GROSS JOKES

What's the difference between a maggot and a cockroach?

Cockroaches crunch more when you eat them.

Why was the stable boy so busy?

Because his work kept piling up.

What do you call a bag of rats?

A rat bag.

What do you get if you cross a dog with a lion?

A terrifed mailman.

Why did the slow skunk cross the road?

To show everyone that he had guts.

ANIMAL GROSSNESS

What did the leech say when there was no more blood left in the dead rat?

"This really sucks."

What do you do if you find a python on the toilet?

You wait until he has finished.

What's black, white, and green?

A zebra with a runny nose.

What do you call a tired bug?

A sleepy-crawly.

Do you know what they say about a bird in the hand?

It will often poop on your wrist.

What do you get if you walk under a cow?

A pat on the head.

What do you call a bug that has worked its way to the top?

Head louse.

What do you call a sleeping bull?

A bull-dozer.

What do you get when you cross a rooster, a dog, and something gross?

Cock-a-poodle-eeew.

What do you get
if you cross a centipede
with a homing pigeon?

A creepy-crawly that
just keeps coming back.

How do fleas
get around?

By itchhiking.

What do you
get when you run
over a parakeet with
a lawnmower?

Shredded tweet.

GROSS JOKES

"Our dog is really lazy."

"Why do you say that?"

"I was watering the garden yesterday and he never lifted a leg to help me."

Why do maggots like open wounds?

They don't have to fight over who gets the scab.

What did one fly ask the other?

"Is this stool taken?"

What do you get if you cross a scorpion with a rose?

I don't know, but don't try smelling it.

What do you do if an elephant eats a rotten egg?

Get out of the way.

ANIMAL GROSSNESS

Oliver goes over to the Hannigans' house for dinner. When he gets there, Mr. Hannigan hasn't yet finished cooking the meat loaf, so Oliver sits on the couch to wait. Unfortunately, he has a terrible case of gas and really needs to fart.

Just then, Rufus, the family dog, jumps up on the couch. Oliver smiles, thinking that if he farts now, everyone will think Rufus was the culprit.

So Oliver lets one rip and Mr. Hannigan yells, "Rufus, get down from the couch."

Oliver's plan had worked, so he decides to squeeze out another fart.

"Rufus, get down," Mr. Hannigan yells again.

Oliver giggles and farts for a third time. Mr. Hannigan comes running in from the kitchen. "Rufus," he says, angrily. "Get down from that couch before Oliver poops all over you."

How do you keep a rooster from crowing on Sunday morning?

Make rooster stew on Saturday night.

Why are frogs always so happy?

They eat whatever bugs them.

What do you get when you cross a chicken with a cement mixer?

A bricklayer.

Which day of the week do fish really hate?

Fry-day.

What did the grasshopper say when it hit the windshield?

"I don't have the guts to do that again."

What do you get when you cross a cow with a camel?

Lumpy milkshakes.

Why aren't elephants allowed on beaches?

They can't keep their trunks up.

How do you find where a flea has bitten you?

You start from scratch.

What do you get when you cross a bug with a boot?

A squashed bug.

What treat do cats like the most?

Chocolate mouse.

What did the dog say to the insect?

"Long time, no flea."

Why are elephants so wrinkly?

Because they're too difficult to iron.

What do you get if you cross a worm and a young goat?

A dirty kid.

MWAH-HA-HA MONSTERS

We all love to be spooked by monsters. Their gross obsessions like sucking blood and haunting buildings make for funny jokes. Mwah-ha-ha!

What happened to Godzilla after he chewed through the streets of New York?

He came down with a sewer throat.

Which type of dog do ghosts like the most?

A ghoul-den retriever.

What has webbed feet and fangs?

Count Quackula.

What does a vampire order at the bar?

A Bloody Mary.

GROSS JOKES

Why is Dracula's bank account always in the red?

Because it's a blood bank.

Who does Dracula always take to a party?

The girl necks door.

Why do vampires have such a high divorce rate?

Because things never seem to work out when your love is in vein.

MWAH-HA-HA MONSTERS

What do you get when you cross a vampire with a snowman?

Frostbite.

What do ghosts like on their bagels?

Scream cheese.

How do you know when a mummy has raided your fridge?

All the food is unwrapped.

What's green, crunchy, and bites you on the neck?

A vampickle.

How do vampires go sailing?

On blood vessels.

What kind of streets do ghosts like to gather on?

Dead-end streets.

Who did Dracula invite to his wedding?

All his blood relatives.

Did you hear about the skeleton who went on a low-fat milk diet?

Now he's all skim and bones.

What do ghosts eat for dessert?

Ice scream.

What goes "Flap, flap. Bite, bite. Ouch, ouch"?

Dracula with a toothache.

What does Dracula say before going out?

"I'm just popping out for a bite."

MWAH-HA-HA MONSTERS

What do vampires wear in autumn?

Their bat-to-school clothes.

What pets does Dracula own?

A bloodhound and a ghoulfish.

Why was the ghost so embarrassed?

He spook too soon.

What did the monster get when he won the race?

A ghoul medal.

What flowers do ghouls like?

Morning gories.

What side of Godzilla should you stay away from?

The inside.

What kind of letter does Dracula get from admirers?

Fang mail.

What do you call a gremlin on crutches?

A hobblin' goblin.

Why are robots never afraid?

Because they have nerves of steel.

Why did the ghost cross the road?

To get to "the other side."

Do werewolves ever argue?

Whenever there's a full moon, they fight tooth and nail.

What food do zombies like the most?

Chicken croak-ettes.

MWAH-HA-HA MONSTERS

Why did the zombie twins stay home from school?

They were feeling rotten.

How can you tell when a vampire has been in a bakery?

All the filling from the jelly doughnuts is missing.

What's the most important day in ancient Egypt?

Mummy's Day.

What do ghosts do on their days off?

Housecreeping.

Why did the art teacher praise Dracula?

Because he was good at drawing blood.

GROSS JOKES

What kind of sales attract zombies?

Graveyard sales.

Why did the vampire never gain weight?

He ate necks to nothing.

Why do ghosts make such poor football fans?

They spend all their time booing.

What kind of art are ghosts good at?

Ghoulages.

What happened when the vampires had a race?

They were neck and neck.

What overnight shipping company do vampires use?

Necks Day Delivery.

MWAH-HA-HA MONSTERS

Who did the ghost marry?

His ghoulfriend.

Why did Dracula always have breath mints with him?

He had bat breath.

Why was the mummy so tense?

He was all wound up.

What did the mother ghost say to the baby ghost?

"Go and put your boos and shocks on."

What can you find between Godzilla's toes?

Slow runners.

Why do dragons sleep all day?

So they can fight knights.

When do mummies eat breakfast?

When they catch you.

What happened when the wizard turned a boy into a hare?

He wouldn't stop rabbiting on about it.

Why did the skeleton play the piano?

Because he didn't have an organ.

BURPS AND FARTS

**Who doesn't love a smelly joke?
Burps, belches, poop, armpits, feet, and
farts are just some of the stinky things that
gross us out and make us laugh.**

Pardon me for
being so rude.
It was not me,
it was my food.
It just popped up
to say hello.
Now it's gone back
down below.

I sat next
to a duchess at tea,
and it was just as
I feared it would be.
Her rumbling abdominal
was simply phenomenal,
and everyone thought it
was me.

GROSS JOKES

"I'm going to have to let one rip. Do you mind?"

"Not if you don't mind when I throw up."

What do you call "fart" in German?

Farfrompoopin.

How did the astronaut suffocate?

He farted in his spacesuit.

Where is a fart on the color spectrum?

Right after burple.

What's the only kind of poop that doesn't smell terrible?

Shampoo.

What is it called when the queen farts?

Noble gas.

How can you tell when your armpits are stinky?

Your teacher gives you an "A" for not raising your hand in class.

What did one burp say to the other burp?

"Let's be stinkers and come out the other end."

How is a quiet, eggy fart like a ninja?

It's silent but deadly.

What did the queen bee do after she farted?

Issued a royal pardon.

How do you cope with a gas leak?

Leave the room and open all the windows.

A man let out a huge, loud burp. Nearby, a man said, "How dare you burp before my wife?" The burper replied, "I'm sorry. I didn't know she wanted to go first."

What's the easiest thing to break?

Wind.

What do you call a knight who has just eaten baked beans?

Sir Farts-a-lot.

Did you hear about the man who ate a hundred tins of baked beans?

He had a fart attack.

What is invisible and smells like milk and cookies?

Santa's burps.

BURPS AND FARTS

Laugh and the whole world laughs with you. Fart and they'll stop laughing.

Rose: "Ewww, gross. Why did you just burp?"

Owen: "My fart got lonely."

What do you call a fart?

A turd honking for the right of way.

KNOCK, KNOCK!

Who's there?

Smell mop.

Smell mop who?

Ewww. What did you just say?

What did the judge say when the skunk walked into the courtroom?

"Odor in the court."

What do stinky toddlers learn at preschool?

Their one, poo, threes.

BURPS AND FARTS

What did the smelly boy draw in his Valentine's Day card?

Lovefarts.

What did the bird say to its fart?

"You're the wind beneath my wings."

Molly: "Mommy, I hate my sister's guts."

Mom: "Well, stop eating them, then."

What did the smelliest married couple say in their wedding vows?

"Till death do us fart."

98

GROSS JOKES

What do you get if you eat bad onions and rotten eggs?

Tear gas.

What smells the best at dinner?

Your nose.

Why did the skeleton burp in public?

He didn't have the guts to fart.

PIRATES AND WITCHES

There are some truly gross things about witches and pirates. Peg legs, warts, eye patches, pointy nails, and hook hands just for a start.

What is a witch detective called?

Warlock Holmes.

Where do pirates put their stuff at the gym?

In Davey Jones' locker.

What happened to the witch with an upside-down nose?

Every time she sneezed, her hat blew off.

What is evil and ugly on the inside and green on the outside?

A witch dressed as a cucumber.

Which weapons do pirates like the most?

Daggaaaaaarrrrrrs.

What did the witch cry when her coffee machine broke?

"Brew-hoo."

What movie do pirates watch?

Booty and the Beast.

What internet sensation is popular with pirates?

Planking.

What do witches excel at in school?

Spelling.

Why do pirates not like eating their lunch on the beach?

Because of the sand which is there.

What grades did the pirate get in school?

High "C"s.

Why can't pirates learn the alphabet?

Because they insist there are seven "C"s.

A pirate was being interviewed about his life at sea. The interviewer began speaking. "So, Captain, how did you get your peg leg?"

"I fell one night and broke me ankle. The ship doesn't have a doctor, so we cut it off and put the leg on thar."

The reporter was disappointed as she had expected a more exciting story. Her next question was about why he had a hook for a hand. He responded, "Twas me night to do the cookin', and I wasn't paying attention when cuttin' the food. As we didn't have no doctor to fix me up, we put the hook on thar instead."

Once again, the story had been less exciting than expected. The final question was about the patch on his eye, to which he explained, "I was out on the deck lookin' at the sea when a seagull flew overhead. Its droppings fell clear into me eye."

The reporter was confused. "So that's why you wear a patch over your eye?"

The captain responded, "No, I tried to wipe off the poop with me hook."

What has four hands and four legs?

Eight pirates.

Why did the angry witch land with a bump?

Because she lost her temper and flew off the handle.

How much did the pirate pay for his peg leg and hook?

An arm and a leg.

What do you get when you cross a sorceress with a billionaire?

A very witch person.

Why wouldn't the pirate's phone work?

He left it off the hook.

Why did the witch give up fortune-telling?

She saw no future in it.

What do witches wear to bed?

Frightgowns.

GROSS JOKES

Why couldn't the witch sing Christmas carols?

Because of the frog in her throat.

How do witches tell the time?

With a witch watch.

Which side of a parrot has the prettiest feathers?

The outside.

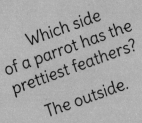

107

Why are pirate flags always in a bad mood?

Because they have cross bones.

Why did the witch itch?

Someone took away the "W."

What did the pirate name his daughter?

Peggy.

Why couldn't the pirate play cards?

He was standing on the deck.

What happened to the witch when she went to another country?

She got broomsick.

What happened to the misbehaving witch at school?

She got exspelled.

KNOCK, KNOCK!

It's impossible to resist saying, "Who's there?" when you hear the words "KNOCK, KNOCK!" These funny jokes use puns and play on words. There is nothing better than a slightly gross KNOCK-KNOCK joke.

KNOCK, KNOCK!

Who's there?

Boo.

Boo who?

Don't cry. It's only a silly joke.

KNOCK, KNOCK!

Who's there?

Butter.

Butter who?

Butter be quick. I need to use the bathroom.

KNOCK, KNOCK!

Who's there?

Hatch.

Hatch who?

Bless you, but I'm all out of tissues.

GROSS JOKES

KNOCK, KNOCK!

Who's there?

Lou.

Loo who?

Loo is free now if you want to pee.

KNOCK, KNOCK!

Who's there?

Ivan.

Ivan who?

Ivan itchy bottom.

KNOCK, KNOCK!

Who's there?

Carl.

Carl who?

Carl a doctor. I just swallowed a leech.

KNOCK, KNOCK!

KNOCK, KNOCK!

Who's there?

Donna.

Donna who?

Donna sit there, someone peed on the seat.

KNOCK, KNOCK!

Who's there?

Gruesome.

Gruesome who?

I like flowers so I gruesome.

KNOCK, KNOCK!

Who's there?

Maggot.

Maggot who?

Maggot is too full.
I'm going to vomit.

KNOCK, KNOCK!

Who's there?

Howie.

Howie who?

Howie going to hide
that disgusting smell?

KNOCK, KNOCK!

Who's there?

Thistle.

Thistle who?

Thistle be the last
chance for maggot pie.

KNOCK, KNOCK!

KNOCK, KNOCK!

Who's there?

Dwayne.

Dwayne who?

Dwayne the bathtub.
I'm dwowning.

KNOCK, KNOCK!

Who's there?

Pearl.

Pearl who?

Pearl-ease stop farting.
You're stinking
up the house.

114

KNOCK, KNOCK!

Who's there?

Howard.

Howard who?

Howard I know the dog would puke if I fed him cat poop?

KNOCK, KNOCK!

Who's there?

Butternut.

Butternut who?

Butternut fall into that steaming pile of horse poop.

KNOCK, KNOCK!

Who's there?

Snot.

Snot who?

Snot nice to keep me waiting outside.

KNOCK, KNOCK!

KNOCK, KNOCK!

Who's there?

Canoe.

Canoe who?

Canoe flush that stinky toilet, please?

KNOCK, KNOCK!

Who's there?

Iliketoeep.

Iliketoeep who?

You like to eat poop?

KNOCK, KNOCK!

Who's there?

Coffin.

Coffin who?

Coffin and sneezing out here.

116

KNOCK, KNOCK!
Who's there?
Snot.
Snot who?
Snot my fault.

KNOCK, KNOCK!
Who's there?
Ozzie.
Ozzie who?
Ozzie you later.
You smell horrible
right now.

KNOCK, KNOCK!
Who's there?
Wendy.
Wendy who?
Wendy you want
to smell my burp?

KNOCK, KNOCK!

Who's there?

Avenue.

Avenue who?

Avenue shut the bathroom door? It stinks in there.

KNOCK, KNOCK!

Who's there?

Wound.

Wound who?

Wound you be my friend?

KNOCK, KNOCK!

Who's there?

Europe.

Europe who?

I'm a poop? That's not very nice.

KNOCK, KNOCK!
Who's there?
Nobody.
Nobody who?
Nobody who?
Nobody who?
Hello? Is anyone there?

KNOCK, KNOCK!
Who's there?
Iceswallop.
Iceswallop who?
Eeeurrrgh! Gross.

RIDDLE ME GROSS

Riddles are a lot of fun to solve. You need to think in different and sometimes creepy ways to get to the answer. All answers for this gross section are on pages 128 and 129.

1. What has to be broken before you can use it?

2. What has a thumb and four fingers but is not alive?

GROSS JOKES

3. What has a neck but no head?

4. Everyone has it and no one can lose it. What is it?

5. Why did the boy bury his flashlight?

6. Poor people have it, rich people need it. If you eat it you die. What is it?

7. What is as light as a feather, but even the world's strongest person couldn't hold it for a very long time?

8. What is so delicate that saying its name breaks it?

10. A frog jumped into a pot of cream and started treading. He soon felt something solid under his feet and was able to hop out of the pot. What did the frog feel under his feet?

9. What has one eye but cannot see?

11. They come out at night without being called and are lost in the day without being stolen. What are they?

12. What has a head but never weeps, has a bed but never sleeps, can run but never walks, and has a bank but no money?

13. Can you name three consecutive days without saying Tuesday, Friday, or Sunday?

14. What can you hear but not touch or see?

15. What loses its head in the morning but gets it back at night?

16. What kind of room has no doors or windows?

17. I have keys but no locks. I have space but no room. You can enter, but can't go outside. What am I?

18. What two things can you never eat for breakfast?

19. Weight in my stomach, trees on my back, nails in my ribs, it's feet I lack. What am I?

20. I am very easy to get into, but it's very hard to get out of me. What am I?

21. All things I devour: birds, beasts, trees, flowers. I gnaw iron and bite steel. I grind hard stones to meal. What am I?

22. I have a tongue but cannot taste. I have a soul but cannot feel. What am I?

23. What can you keep but give away at the same time?

24. What runs but has no legs?

25. What has a hole but still holds water?

26. What has arms and legs but no body?

27. What has a head and a tail but no body?

RIDDLE ME GROSS

Answers

1. An egg.

2. A glove.

3. A bottle.

4. A shadow.

5. Because the batteries died.

6. Nothing.

7. Breath.

8. Silence.

9. A needle.

10. The frog felt butter under his feet because he churned the cream and made butter.

11. Stars.

12. A river.

13. Yesterday, today, and tomorrow.

GROSS JOKES

14. Your voice.

15. A pillow.

16. A mushroom.

17. A keyboard.

18. Lunch and dinner.

19. A ship.

20. Trouble.

21. Time.

22. A shoe.

23. A cold.

24. A tap.

25. A toilet.

26. A chair.

27. A coin.

TOILET JOKES

The toilet is a ripe area for jokes. Just think of all the horrible, loud, and smelly things that happen in the toilet. Get ready to laugh at the grossness of those stinky bathroom bowls.

Which king has the noisiest bottom?

King Richard the Lion-fart.

Mel: "Do you know anyone who has been on the TV?"

Andrew: "My brother did once, but he uses the toilet now."

GROSS JOKES

Why do idiots whistle when they go poop?

So they can remember which end to wipe.

Why did the boy take toilet paper to the birthday party?

Because he was a party pooper.

A boy with a bladder problem asked his teacher if he could go to the bathroom.

"Only if you recite the alphabet," answered the teacher.

"Okay," said the boy. "ABCDEFGHIJK LMNO - QRSTUV WXYZ."

"Where's the 'P'?" asked the teacher.

"Running down my leg," said the boy.

131

What did the first mate see in the spaceship's toilet?

The captain's log.

Why did the toilet paper roll down the hill?

Because it wanted to get to the bottom.

What did one piece of toilet paper say to the other piece?

"I can't tear myself away from you."

132

What did Shakespeare say when he was potty training?

"To pee or not to pee. That is the question."

Did you hear about the new principal who's been keeping the boys on their toes?

He raised all the urinals six inches.

What did the bath say when he thought the toilet was ill?

"You look flushed."

Why was the toilet paper unimpressed with the price?

It felt it was ripped off.

What goes ho, ho, ho, plop, plop, plop?

Santa on the toilet.

Has the bottom fallen out of your world?

Eat prunes, and then the world will fall out of your bottom.

What is a woman with two toilets on her head called?

Lulu.

What vegetable can you find in a toilet?

A leek.

134

What happened when the girl ate too many Mexican jumping beans?

Her poop hopped right out of the toilet.

Carl: "Teacher, do farts have lumps?"

Teacher: "Um, no."

Carl: "Then I definitely just pooped my pants."

Jen entered a competition where the first prize was a toilet and the last prize was a toilet.

It was a win-loos situation.

Why did the man bring the bowling ball into the bathroom?

So he could watch his toilet bowl.

What's green and lives at the bottom of the toilet?

Kermit the bog.

Why did the mummy go to the toilet?

To wrap itself in toilet paper, of course.

Three boys were at the top of the slide when a genie appeared, saying it would grant them each one wish, which would come true at the bottom of the slide. They just had to call out their wish as they went down the slide.

The first boy shouted, "Money," as he went down the slide and he landed in a huge pile of money.

The second boy shouted, "Chocolate," as he went down the slide and was surrounded by chocolate at the bottom.

The third boy exclaimed, "Weeeeee," as he went down the slide . . . and he landed in a puddle of stinky, yellow wee.

TOILET JOKES

What do you call a nut that has to use the bathroom?

A pee-nut.

What do you call an igloo without a toilet?

An ig.

138

GROSS JOKES

Why can't you hear a pterodactyl go to the bathroom?

Because it has a silent "P."

Have you heard the joke about the toilet?

Never mind, it's too dirty.

Which continent are you from while sitting on a toilet?

Euro-peein'.

What happened when the toilet paper crossed the road?

It got stuck in the crack.

HAVE YOU HEARD THIS ONE?

Just when you think we've told all the gross jokes, we find some more! Here are some gross jokes that you might not have heard.

Did you hear about my cousin Gus?

He let one go and stank the bus.

GROSS JOKES

What do you call a deer with no eyes?

No idea.

What do you call a deer with no eyes and no legs?

Still no idea.

Did you hear about the constipated mathematician?

He worked it out with a pencil.

What do you call a man with a shovel in his head?

Doug.

What do you call a man without a shovel in his head?

Douglas.

141

HAVE YOU HEARD THIS ONE?

Have you heard about the two ghosts who fell madly in love?

It was love at first fright.

Have you heard about the teacher who married a dairymaid?

It didn't last. They were like chalk and cheese.

What's black, white, and red all over?

A constipated zebra trying to poop.

GROSS JOKES

Have you heard about the cat who drank three bowls of milk?

He set a new lap record.

Have you heard about the hungry clock?

It went back four seconds.

Have you heard about the two satellite dishes that got married?

The wedding was terrible, but the reception was great.

SMELL YOU LATER!